North American Birds Picture Book

JACQUELINE MELGREN

Northern Cardinal

Black-Capped Chickadee

Baltimore Oriole

Eastern Bluebird

Downy Woodpecker

American Goldfinch

Cactus Wren

Blue Jay

Eastern Brown Pelican

Rose Breasted Grosbeak

Indigo Bunting

House Finch

Cedar Waxwing

Dark-Eyed Junco

American Robin

Montezuma Quail

Yellow Warbler

Tufted Titmouse

Ruby-Throated Hummingbird

Barred Owl

Elegant Tern

Mourning Dove

Elegant Trogon

White Breasted Nuthatch

Killdeer

Bald Eagle

Red-winged Blackbird

Emperor Goose

Greater Roadrunner

Horned Puffin

www.ingramcontent.com/pod-product-compliance
Ingram Content Group UK Ltd.
Pitfield, Milton Keynes, MK11 3LW, UK
UKHW060114300726
14090UKWH00002B/180

* 9 7 8 9 1 8 9 4 5 2 3 9 8 *